REMINISCENCES OF

LEO NICOLAYEVICH TOLSTOY

By
MAXIM GORKY

Authorized Translation from the Russian

by
S. S. KOTELIANSKY

and
LEONARD WOOLF

TRANSLATORS' NOTE TO SECOND EDITION

Reminiscences of Leo Nicolayevitch Tolstoi, by Maxim Gorky, was originally published in Russian in Petrograd in 1919. The first half of the book, consisting of notes, had been written between 1900 and 1901, when Tolstoi, Gorky, and Tchekhov were living in the Crimea. The second half consists of a letter written by Gorky in 1910.

A second edition of the book will shortly be published in Russia, and will contain a few additional notes not included in the first edition. We have included this additional matter in the present edition, enclosing it in square brackets.

PREFACE

This little book is composed of fragmentary notes written by me during the period when I lived in Oleise and Leo Nicolayevitch at Gaspra in the Crimea. They cover the period of Tolstoi's serious illness and of his subsequent recovery. The notes were carelessly jotted down on scraps of paper, and I thought I had lost them, but recently I have found some of them. Then I have also included here an unfinished letter written by me under the influence of the "going away" of Leo Nicolayevitch from Yassnaya Polyana, and of his death. I publish the letter just as it was written at the time, and without correcting a single word. And I do not finish it, for somehow or other this is not possible. M. GORKY.

NOTES

I

The thought which beyond others most often and conspicuously gnaws at him is the thought of God. At moments it seems, indeed, not to be a thought, but a violent resistance to something which he feels above him. He speaks of it less than he would like, but thinks of it always. It can scarcely be said to be a sign of old age, a presentiment of death—no, I think that it comes from his exquisite human pride, and—a bit—from a sense of humiliation: for, being Leo Tolstoi, it is humiliating to have to submit one's will to a streptococcus. If he were a scientist, he would certainly evolve the most ingenious hypotheses, make great discoveries.

II

H3e has wonderful hands—not beautiful, but knotted with swollen veins, and yet full of a singular expressiveness and the power of creativeness. Probably Leonardo da Vinci had hands like that. With such hands one can do anything. Sometimes, when talking, he will move his fingers, gradually close them into a fist, and then, suddenly opening them, utter a good, full-weight word. He is like a god, not a Sabaoth or Olympian, but the kind of Russian god who "sits on a maple throne under a golden lime tree," not very majestic, but perhaps more cunning than all the other gods.

III

He treats Sulerzhizky with the tenderness of a woman. For Tchekhov his love is paternal—in this love is the feeling of the pride of a creator—Suler rouses in him just tenderness, a perpetual interest and rapture which never seems to weary the sorcerer. Perhaps there is something a little ridiculous in this feeling, like the love of an old maid for a parrot, a pug dog, or a tom-cat. Suler is a fascinatingly wild bird from some strange unknown land. A hundred men like him could change the face, as well as the soul, of a provincial town. Its face they would smash and its soul they would fill with a passion for riotous, brilliant, headstrong wildness. One loves Suler easily and gaily, and when I see how carelessly women accept him, they surprise and anger me. Yet under this carelessness is hidden, perhaps, caution. Suler is not reliable. What will he do to-morrow? He may throw a bomb or he may join a troupe of public-house minstrels. He has energy enough for three lifetimes, and fire of life—so much that he seems to sweat sparks like over-heated iron.

IIIa

[But once he got thoroughly cross with Suler. Suler inclined to anarchism, and often argued with bitterness about the freedom of the individual. In such cases Leo Nicolayevitch always chaffed him.

I remember that Suler once got hold of a thin little pamphlet by Prince Kropotkin; he flamed up, and all day long explained to everyone the wisdom of anarchism, overwhelming them with his philosophizing.

"Oh, stop it, Liovushka," said Leo Nicolayevitch irritably, "you are annoying. You hammer away like a parrot at one word, freedom, freedom; but what is the sense of it? If you attained your freedom, what do you imagine would happen? In the philosophic sense, a bottomless void, and in actual life you would become an idler, a parasite. If you were free in your sense, what would bind you to life or to people? Now, birds are free, but still they build nests; you, however, wouldn't even build a nest, but would gratify your sexual feeling anywhere, like a dog. You think seriously, and you will come to see, you will come to feel, that this freedom is ultimately emptiness, boundlessness."

He frowned angrily, was silent for a while, and then added quietly, "Christ was free and so was Buddha, and both took on themselves the sins of the world and voluntarily entered the prison of earthly life. Further than that nobody has gone, nobody. And you—we—well, what's the good of talking—we are all looking for freedom from obligations towards our fellow men, whereas it is just that feeling of our obligations which has made us men, and, if those obligations were not there, we should live like the beasts."

He smiled. "And now here we are arguing how we ought to live. The result isn't very great, but it is something. For instance, you are arguing with me, and are getting so cross that you are going blue in the nose, yet you don't hit me, you don't even swear at me. But if you really felt free, you'd kill me on the spot, and there'd be an end of it." After a silence, he added: "Freedom consists in all and everything agreeing with me, but in that case I don't exist, because we are only conscious of ourselves in conflicts and contradictions,"]

IV

Goldenweiser played Chopin, which called forth these remarks from Leo Nicolayevitch: "A certain German princeling said: 'Where you want to have slaves, there you should have as much music as possible.' That's a true thought, a true observation—music dulls the mind. Especially do the Catholics realize that; our priests, of course, won't reconcile themselves to Mendelssohn in church. A Tula priest assured me that Christ was not a Jew, though the son of the Jewish God and his mother a Jewess—he did admit that, but says he: 'It's impossible.' I asked him: 'But how then? 'He shrugged his shoulders and said: 'That's just the mystery.'"

V

"An intellectual is like the old Galician Prince Vladimirko, who, as far back as the twelfth century, 'boldly' declared: 'There are no miracles in our time.' Six hundred years have passed and all the intellectuals hammer away at each other: 'There are no miracles, there are no miracles.' And all the people believe in miracles, just as they did in the twelfth century."

VI

"The minority feel the need of God because they have got everything else, the majority because they have nothing."

I would put it differently: the majority believe in God from cowardice, only the few believe in him from fullness of soul.

VIa

"You like Andersen's Tales?" he asked thoughtfully. "I couldn't make them out when they first appeared in the translation of Marko Vovtchok, but about ten years later I took up the book and read it, and suddenly realized with great clearness that Andersen was very lonely—very. I don't know about his life, but he seems to have lived loosely and to have travelled a great deal, but that only confirms my feeling that he was lonely. And because of that he addressed himself to the young, although it's a mistake to imagine that children pity a man more than grown-ups do. Children pity nothing; they do not know what pity is."

VII

He advised me to read Buddhistic scriptures. Of Buddhism and Christ he always speaks sentimentally. When he speaks about Christ, it is always peculiarly poor, no enthusiasm, no feeling in his words, and no spark of real fire. I think he regards Christ as simple and deserving of pity, and, although at times he admires Him, he hardly loves Him. It is as though he were uneasy: if Christ came to a Russian village, the girls might laugh at Him.

VIII

To-day the Grand Duke Nicolay Mikhailovitch was at Tolstoi's, evidently a very clever man. His behaviour is very modest; he talks little. He has sympathetic eyes and a fine figure, quiet gestures. Leo Nicolayevitch smiled caressingly at him, and spoke now French, now English. In Russian he said:—

"Karamzin wrote for the Tsar, Soloviov long and tediously, and Klutchevsky for his own amusement. Cunning fellow Klutchevsky: at first you get the impression that he is praising, but as you read on, you see that he is blaming."

Someone mentioned Zabielin.

"He's nice. An amateur collector, he collects everything, whether it is useful or not. He describes food as if he had never had a square meal; but he is very, very amusing."

IX

He reminds me of those pilgrims who all their life long, stick in hand, walk the earth, travelling thousands of miles from one monastery to another, from one saint's relics to another, terribly homeless and alien to all men and things. The world is not for them, nor God either. They pray to Him from habit, and in their secret soul they hate Him—why does He drive them over the earth from one end to the other? What for? People are stumps, roots, stones on the path; one stumbles over them, and sometimes is hurt by them. One can do without them, but it is pleasant sometimes to surprise a man with one's own unlikeness to him, to show one's difference from him.

X

"Friedrich of Prussia said very truly: 'Everyone must save himself in his own way.' He also said: 'Argue as much as you like, but obey.' But when dying he confessed: 'I have grown weary of ruling slaves.' So-called great men are always terribly contradictory: that is forgiven them with all their other follies. Though contradictoriness is not folly: a fool is stubborn, but does not know how to contradict himself. Yes, Friedrich was a strange man: among the Germans he won the reputation of being the best king, yet he could not bear them; he disliked even Goethe and Wieland."

XI

"Romanticism comes from the fear of looking straight into the eyes of truth," he said yesterday with regard to Balmont's poems. Suler disagreed with him and, lisping with excitement, read very feelingly some more poems.

"These, Liovushka, are not poems; they are charlatanism, rubbish, as people said in the Middle Ages, a nonsensical stringing together of words. Poetry is art-less; when Fet wrote:

'I know not myself what I will sing,
But only my song is ripening,'

he expressed a genuine, real, people's sense of poetry. The peasant, too, doesn't know that he's a poet—oh, oi, ah, and aye—and there comes off a real song, straight from the soul, like a bird's. These new poets of yours are inventing. There are certain silly French things called articles de Paris—well, that's what your stringers of verses produce. Nekrassov's miserable verses, too, are invented from beginning to end."

"And Béranger?" Suler asked.

"Béranger—that's quite different. What's there in common between the French and us? They are sensualists; the life of the spirit is not as important to them as the flesh. To a Frenchman woman is everything. They are a worn-out, emasculated people. Doctors say that all consumptives are sensualists."

Suler began to argue with his peculiar directness, pouring out a random flood of words. Leo Nicolayevitch looked at him and said with a broad smile:

"You are peevish to-day, like a girl who has reached the age when she should marry but has no lover."

XII

The illness dried him up still more, burnt something out of him. Inwardly he seemed to become lighter, more transparent, more resigned. His eyes are still keener, his glance piercing. He listens attentively as though recalling something which he has forgotten or as though waiting for something new and unknown. In Yassnaya Polyana he seemed to me a man who knew everything and had nothing more to learn—a man who had settled every question.

XIII

If he were a fish, he would certainly swim only in the ocean, never coming to the narrow seas, and particularly not to the flat waters of earthly rivers. Around him here there rest or dart hither and thither the little fishes: what he says does not interest them, is not necessary to them, and his silence does not frighten or move them. Yet his silence is impressive like that of a real hermit driven out from this world. Though he speaks a great deal and as a duty upon certain subjects, his silence is felt to be still greater. Certain things one cannot tell to anyone. Surely he has some thoughts of which he is afraid.

XIV

Someone sent him an excellent version of the story of Christ's godson. He read it aloud with pleasure to Suler,

Tchekhov—he read amazingly well. He was especially amused by the devils torturing the landowners. There was something which I did not like in that. He cannot be insincere, but, if this be sincere, then it makes it worse. Then he said:

"How well the peasants compose stories. Everything is simple, the words few, and a great deal of feeling. Real wisdom uses few words; for instance, 'God have mercy on us.'"

Yet the story is a cruel one.

XV

His interest in me is ethnological. In his eyes I belong to a species not familiar to him—only that.

XVI

I read my story "The Bull" to him. He laughed much, and praised my knowledge of "the tricks of the language."

"But your treatment of words is not skilful; all your peasants speak cleverly. In actual life what they say is silly and incoherent, and at first you cannot make out what a peasant wants to say. That is done deliberately; under the silliness of their words is always concealed a desire to allow the other person to show what is in his mind. A good peasant will never show at once what is in his own mind: it is not profitable. He knows that people approach a stupid man frankly and directly, and that's the very thing he wants. You stand revealed before him and he at once sees all your weak points. He is suspicious; he is afraid to tell his inmost thoughts even to his wife. But with your peasants in every story everything is revealed: it's a universal council of wisdom. And they all speak in aphorisms; that's not true to life, either; aphorisms are not natural to the Russian language."

"What about sayings and proverbs?"

"That's a different thing. They are not of to-day's manufacture."

"But you yourself often speak in aphorisms."

"Never. There again you touch everything up; people as well as nature—especially people. So did Lieskov, an affected, finicking writer whom nobody reads now. Don't let anyone influence you, fear no one, and then you'll be all right."

XVII

In his diary which he gave me to read, I was struck by a strange aphorism: "God is my desire."

To-day, on returning him the book, I asked him what it meant.

"An unfinished thought," he said, glancing at the page and screwing up his eyes. "I must have wanted to say: 'God is my desire to know Him.' ... No, not that ..." He began to laugh, and, rolling up the book into a tube, he put it into the big pocket of his blouse. With God he has very suspicious relations; they sometimes remind me of the relation of "two bears in one den."

XVIII

On science:

"Science is a bar of gold made by a charlatan alchemist. You want to simplify it, to make it accessible to all: you find that you have coined a lot of false coins.. When the people realize the real value of those coins, they won't thank you."

XIX

We walked in the Yussopov Park. He spoke superbly about the customs of the Moscow aristocracy. A big Russian peasant woman was working on the flower-bed, bent at right angles, showing her ivory legs, shaking her ten-pound breasts. He looked at her attentively.

"It is those caryatids who have kept all that magnificence and extravagance going. Not only by the labour of peasant men and women, not only by the taxes they pay, but in the literal sense by their blood. If the aristocracy had not from time to time mated with such horse-women as she, they would have died out long ago. It is impossible with impunity to waste one's strength, as the young men of my time did. But after sowing their wild oats, many married serf-girls and produced a good breed. In that way, too, the peasant's strength saved them. That strength is everywhere in place. Half the aristocracy always has to spend its strength on itself, and the other half to dilute itself with peasant blood and thus diffuse the peasant blood a little. It's useful."

XX

OF women he talks readily and much, like a French novelist, but always with the coarseness of a Russian peasant. Formerly it used to affect me unpleasantly. To-day in the Almond Park he asked Anton Tchekhov:

"You whored a great deal when you were young?"

Anton Pavlovitch, with a confused smile, and pulling at his little beard, muttered something inaudible, and Leo Nicolayevitch, looking at the sea, confessed:

"I was an indefatigable...."

He said this penitently, using at the end of the sentence a salty peasant word. And I noticed for the first time how simply he used the word, as though he knew no more fitting one to use. All those kinds of words, coming from his shaggy lips, sound simple and natural and lose their soldierly coarseness and filth. I remember my first meeting with him and his talk about "Varienka Oliessova" and "Twenty-six and

One." From the ordinary point of view what he said was a string of indecent words. I was perplexed by it and even offended. I thought that he considered me incapable of understanding any other kind of language. I understand now: it was silly to have felt offended.

XXI

He sat on the stone bench in the shade of the cypresses, looking very lean, small and grey, and yet resembling Sabaoth, who is a little tired and is amusing himself by trying to whistle in tune with a chaffinch. The bird sang in the darkness of the thick foliage: he peered up at it, screwing up his sharp little eyes, and, pursing his lips like a child, he whistled incompetently.

"What a furious little creature. It's in a rage. What bird is it?"

I told him about the chaffinch and its characteristic jealousy.

"All life long one song," he said, "and yet jealous. Man has a thousand songs in his heart and is yet blamed for jealousy; is it fair?" He spoke musingly, as though asking himself questions. "There are moments when a man says to a woman more than she ought to know about him. He speaks and forgets, but she remembers. Perhaps jealousy comes from the fear of degrading one's soul, of being humiliated and ridiculous? Not that a woman is dangerous who holds a man by his ... but she who holds him by his soul...."

When I pointed out the contradiction in this with his "Kreutzer Sonata," the radiance of a sudden smile beamed through his beard, and he said:

"I am not a chaffinch."

In the evening, while walking, he suddenly said: "Man survives earthquakes, epidemics, the horrors of disease, and all the agonies of the soul, but for all time his most tormenting tragedy has been, is, and will be—the tragedy of the bedroom."

Saying this, he smiled triumphantly: at times he has the broad, calm smile of a man who has overcome something extremely difficult or from whom some sharp, long-gnawing pain has lifted suddenly. Every thought burrows into his soul like a tick; he either tears it out at once or allows it to have its fill of his blood, and then, when full, it just drops off of itself.

He read to Suler and me a variant of the scene of the fall of "Father Sergius"—a merciless scene. Suler pouted and fidgeted uneasily.

"What's the matter? Don't you like it?" Leo Nicolayevitch asked.

"It's too brutal, as though from Dostoevsky. She is a filthy girl, and her breasts like pancakes, and all that. Why didn't he sin with a beautiful, healthy woman?"

"That would be sin without justification; as it is, there is justification in pity for the girl. Who could desire her as she is?"

"I cannot make it out...."

"There's a great deal, Liovushka, which you can't make out: you're not shrewd...."

There came in Andrey Lvovitch's wife, and the conversation was interrupted. As she and Suler went out, Leo Nicolayevitch said to me: "Leopold is the purest man I know. He is like that: if he did something bad, it would be out of pity for someone."

XXII

He talks most of God, of peasants, and of woman; of literature rarely and little, as 'though literature were something alien to him. Woman, in my opinion, he regards with implacable hostility and loves to punish her, unless she be a Kittie or Natasha Rostov, i.e., a creature not too narrow. It is the hostility of the male who has not succeeded in getting all the pleasure he could, or it is the hostility of spirit against "the degrading impulses of the flesh." But it is hostility, and cold, as in Anna Karenin. Of "the degrading impulses of the flesh" he spoke well on Sunday in a conversation with Tchekhov and Yelpatievsky about Rousseau's Confession. Suler wrote down what he said, and later, while preparing coffee, burnt it in the spirit-lamp. Once before he burnt Leo Nicolayevitch's opinions on Ibsen, and he also lost the notes of the conversation in which Leo Nicolayevitch said very pagan things on the symbolism of the marriage ritual, agreeing to a certain extent with V. V. Rosanov.

XXIII

In the morning some "stundists" came to Tolstoi from Feodosia, and to-day all day long he spoke about peasants with rapture.

At lunch: "They came both so strong and fleshy; says one: 'Well, we've come uninvited,' and the other says: 'With God's help we shall leave unbeaten,'" and he broke out into child-like laughter, shaking all over.

After lunch, on the terrace:

"We shall soon cease completely to understand the language of the people. Now we say: 'The theory of progress,' 'the role of the individual in history,' 'the evolution of science and a peasant says: 'You can't hide an awl in a sack,' and all theories, histories, evolutions become pitiable and ridiculous, because they are incomprehensible and unnecessary to the people.' But the peasant is stronger than we; he is more tenacious of life, and there may happen to us what happened to the tribe of Atzurs, of whom it was reported to a scholar:

'All the Atzurs have died out, but there is a parrot here who knows a few words of their language.'"
XXIV

"With her body woman is more sincere than man, but with her mind she lies. And when she lies, she does not believe herself; but Rousseau lied and believed his lies."
XXV

"Dostoevsky described one of his mad characters as living and taking vengeance on himself and others because he had served a cause in which he did not believe. He wrote that about himself; that is, he could have said the same of himself."
XXVI

"Some of the words used in church are amazingly obscure: what meaning is there, for instance, in the words: 'The earth is God's and the fulness thereof'? That is not Holy Scripture, but a kind of popular scientific materialism."

"But you explained the words somewhere," said Suler.

"Many things are explained.... 'An explanation does not go up to the hilt.'"

And he gave a cunning little smile.
XXVII

He likes putting difficult and malicious questions:
What do you think of yourself?
Do you love your wife?
Do you think my son, Leo, has talent?
How do you like Sophie Andreyevna?[1]
Once he asked: "Are you fond of me, Alexey Maximovitch?"

This is the maliciousness of a "bogatyr"[2]: Vaska Buslayev played such pranks in his youth, mischievous fellow. He is experimenting, all the time testing something, as if he were going to fight. It is interesting, but not much to my liking. He is the devil, and I am still a babe, and he should leave me alone.

[1] Tolstoi's wife.

[2] A hero in Russian legend, brave, but wild and self-willed like a child.

XXVIII

Perhaps peasant to him means merely—bad smell. He always feels it, and involuntarily has to talk of it.

Last night I told him of my battle with General Kornet's wife; he laughed until he cried, and he got a pain in his side and groaned and kept on crying out in a thin scream:

"With the shovel! On the bottom with the shovel, eh? Right on the bottom! Was it a broad shovel?"

Then, after a pause, he said seriously: "It was generous in you to strike her like that; any other man would have struck her on the head for that. Very generous! You understood that she wanted you?"

"I don't remember. I hardly think that I can have understood."

"Well now! But it's obvious. Of course she wanted you."

"I did not live for that then."

"Whatever you may live for, it's all the same. You are evidently not much of a lady's man. Anyone else in your place would have made his fortune out of the situation, would have become a landed proprietor and have ended by making one of a pair of drunkards."

After a silence:

"You are funny—don't be offended—very funny. And it's very strange that you should still be good-natured when you might well be spiteful ... Yes, you might well be spiteful ... You're strong ... that's good...."

And after another silence, he added thoughtfully: "Your mind I don't understand—it's a very tangled mind—but your heart is sensible ... yes, a sensible heart."

NOTE.—When I lived in Kazan, I entered the service of General Kornet's wife as doorkeeper and gardener. She was a Frenchwoman, a general's widow, a young woman, fat, and with the tiny feet of a little girl. Her eyes were amazingly beautiful, restless and always greedily alert. Before her marriage she was, I think, a huckstress or a cook or, possibly, even a woman of the town. She would get drunk early in the morning and come out in the yard or garden dressed only in a chemise with an orange-coloured gown over it, in Tartar slippers made of red morocco, and on her head a mane of thick hair. Her hair, carelessly done, hung about her red cheeks and shoulders. A young witch! She used to walk about the garden, humming French songs and watching me work, and every now and then she would go to the kitchen window and call:

"Pauline, give me something."

"Something" always meant the same thing—a glass of wine with ice in it.

In the basement of her house there lived three young ladies, the Princesses D. G., whose mother was dead and whose father, a Commissariat-General, had gone off elsewhere. General Kornet's widow took a dislike to the girls and tried to get rid of them by doing every kind of offensive thing to them. She spoke Russian badly, but swore superbly, like an expert drayman. I very much disliked her attitude towards these harmless girls—they looked so sad, frightened, and defenceless. One afternoon, two of them were walking in the garden when suddenly the General's widow appeared, drunk as usual, and began to shout at them to drive them out of the garden. They began walking silently away, but the General's widow stood in the gateway, completely blocking it with her body like a cork, and started swearing at them and using Russian words like a regular drayman. I asked her to stop swearing and let the girls go out, but she shouted: "You, I know you! You get through their window at night."

I was angry, and, taking her by the shoulders, pushed her away from the gate; but she broke away and, facing me, quickly undid her dress, lifted up her chemise, and shouted:—

"I'm nicer than those rats."

Then I lost my temper. I took her by the neck, turned her round, and struck her with my shovel below the back, so that she skipped out of the gate and ran across the yard, crying out three times in great surprise: "O! O! O!"

After that, I got my passport from her confidant, Pauline—also a drunken but very wily woman—took my bundle under my arm, and left the place; and the General's widow, standing at the window with a red shawl in her hand, shouted:—

"I won't call the police—it's all right—listen—come back—don't be afraid."

XXIX

I asked him: "Do you agree with Poznyshiev[1] when he says that doctors have destroyed and are destroying thousands and hundreds of thousands of people?"

"Are you very interested to know?"

"Very."

"Then I shan't tell you."

And he smiled, playing with his thumbs.

I remember in one of his stories he makes a comparison between a quack village vet. and a doctor of medicine:—

"The words 'giltchak,' 'potchetchny,' bloodletting,'[2] are they not precisely the same as nerves, rheumatism, organisms, etc.?"

And this was written after Jenner, Behring, Pasteur. It is perversity!

[1] In Kreutzer Sonata.

[2] Words used by quack vets, for the diseases of horses.

XXX

How strange that he is so fond of playing cards. He plays seriously, passionately. His hands become nervous when he takes the cards up, exactly as if he were holding live birds instead of inanimate pieces of cardboard.

XXXI

"Dickens said a very clever thing: 'Life is given to us on the definite understanding that we boldly defend it to the last.' On the whole, he was a sentimental, loquacious, and not very clever writer, but he knew how to construct a novel as no one else could, certainly better than Balzac. Someone has said: 'Many are possessed by the passion for writing books, but few are ashamed of them afterwards.' Balzac was not ashamed, nor was Dickens, and both of them wrote quite a number of bad books. Still, Balzac is a genius. Or at any rate the thing which you can only call genius...."

XXXIa

[Someone brought Leo Tikhomirov's book, Why I Ceased to be a Revolutionary: Leo Nicolayevitch took the book from the table, waved it in the air, and said: "What he says here about political murder is good, that there is no clear idea in that method. The idea, says a frenzied murderer, can only be anarchical sovereignty of the individual and contempt for society and for mankind. That is true, but 'anarchical sovereignty 'is a slip of the pen, it should have been 'monarchical.' That is a good and true idea; all the terrorists will trip up over it—I mean the honest ones. The man who naturally loves killing won't trip up. There is nothing for him to trip up over. He's just a plain murderer, and has only accidentally become a terrorist."]

XXXII

Sometimes he seems to be conceited and intolerant, like a Volga preacher, and this is terrible in a man who is the sounding bell of this world. Yesterday he said to me:

"I am more of a mouzhik than you and I feel better in a mouzhik way."

God, he ought not to boast of it, he must not!

XXXIII

I read him some scenes from my play, The Lower Depths; he listened attentively and then asked:

"Why do you write that?"

I explained as best I could.

"One always notices that you jump like a cock on to everything. And more—you always want to paint all the grooves and cracks over with your own paint. You remember that Andersen says: 'The gilt will come off and the pig-skin will remain'; just as our peasants say: 'Everything will pass away, the truth alone will remain.' You'd much better not put the plaster on, for you yourself will suffer for it later. Again, your language is very skilful, with all kinds of tricks—that's no good. You ought to write more simply; people speak simply, even incoherently, and that's good. A peasant doesn't ask: 'Why is a third more than a fourth, if four is always more than three,' as one learned young lady asked. No tricks, please."

He spoke irritably; clearly he disliked very much what I had read to him. And after a silence, looking over my head, he said gloomily:

"Your old man is not sympathetic, one does not believe in his goodness. The actor is all right, he's good. You know Fruits of Enlightenment? My cook there is rather like your actor. Writing plays is difficult. But your prostitute also came off well, they must be like that. Have you known many of them?"

"I used to."

"Yes, one can see that. Truth always shows itself. Most of what you say comes out of yourself, and therefore you have no characters, and all your people have the same face. I should think you don't understand women; they don't come off with you. One does not remember them...."

At this moment A. L.'s wife came in and called us to come to tea, and he got up and went out very quickly, as if he were glad to end the conversation.

XXXIV

"What is the most terrible dream you have ever had?" Tolstoi asked me.

I rarely have dreams and remember them badly, but two have remained in my memory and probably will for the rest of my life.

I dreamt once that I saw the sky scrofulous, putrescent, greenish-yellow, and the stars in it were round, flat, without rays, without lustre, like scabs on the skin of a diseased person. And there glided across this putrescent sky slowly reddish forked lightning, rather like a snake, and when it touched a star the star swelled up into a ball and burst noiselessly, leaving behind it a darkish spot, like a little smoke; and then the spot vanished quickly in the bleared and liquid sky. Thus all the stars one after another burst and perished, and the sky, growing darker and more horrible, at last whirled upwards, bubbled and bursting into fragments began to fall on my head in a kind of cold jelly, and in the spaces between the fragments there appeared a shiny blackness as though of iron. Leo Nicolayevitch said: "Now that comes from a learned book; you must have read something on astronomy; hence the nightmare. And the other dream?"

The other dream: a snowy plain, smooth like a sheet of paper; no hillock, no tree, no bush anywhere, only—barely visible—a few rods poked out from under the snow. And across the snow of this dead desert from horizon to horizon there stretched a yellow strip of a hardly distinguishable road, and over the road there marched slowly a pair of grey felt top boots—empty.

He raised his shaggy, were-wolf eyebrows, looked at me intently and thought for a while.

"That's terrible. Did you really dream that, you didn't invent it? But there's something bookish in it also."

And suddenly he got angry, and said, irritably, sternly, rapping his knee with his finger: "But you're not a drinking man? It's unlikely that you ever drank much. And yet there's something drunken in these dreams. There was a German writer, Hoffmann, who dreamt that card tables ran about the street, and all that sort of thing, but then he was a drunkard— a 'calaholic,' as our literate coachmen say. Empty boots marching—that's really terrible. Even if you did invent it, it's good. Terrible."

Suddenly he gave a broad smile, so that even his cheek bones beamed.

"And imagine this: suddenly, in the Tverskaya street, there runs a card table with its curved legs, its boards clap, clap, raising a chalky dust, and you can even still see the numbers on the green cloth—excise clerks playing whist on it for three days and nights on end—the table could not bear it any longer and ran away."

He laughed, and then, probably noticing that I was a little hurt by his distrust of me:

"Are you hurt because I thought your dreams bookish? Don't be annoyed; sometimes, I know, one invents something without being aware of it, something which one cannot believe, which can't possibly be believed, and then one imagines that one dreamt it and did not invent it at all. There was a story which an old landowner told. He dreamt that he was walking in a wood and came out of it on to a steppe. On the steppe he saw two hills, which suddenly turned into a woman's breasts, and between them rose up a black face which, instead of eyes, had two moons like white spots. The old man dreamt that he was standing between the woman's legs, in front of him a deep, dark ravine, which sucked him in. After the dream his hair began to grow grey and his hands to tremble, and he went abroad to Doctor Kneip to take a water cure. But, really, he must have seen something of the kind—he was a dissolute fellow."

He patted me on the shoulder.

"But you are neither a drunkard nor dissolute—how do you come to have such dreams?"

"I don't know."

"We know nothing about ourselves."

He sighed, screwed up his eyes, thought for a bit, and then added in a low voice: "We know nothing."

This evening, during our walk, he took my arm and said:

"The boots are marching—terrible, eh? Quite empty—tiop, tiop—and the snow scrunching. Yes, it's good; but you are very bookish, very. Don't be cross, but it's bad and will stand in your way."

I am scarcely more bookish than he, and at the time I thought him a cruel rationalist despite all his pleasant little phrases.

XXXV

At times he gives one the impression of having just arrived from some distant country, where people think and feel differently and their relations and language are different. He sits in a corner tired and grey, as though the dust of another earth were on him, and he looks attentively at everything with the look of a foreigner or of a dumb man.

Yesterday, before dinner, he came into the drawing-room, just like that, his thoughts far away. He sat down on the sofa, and, after a moment's silence, suddenly said, swaying his body a little, rubbing the palm of his hand on his knee, and wrinkling up his face:

"Still that is not all—not all."

Someone, always stolidly stupid as a flat-iron, asked: "What do you say?"

He looked at him fixedly, and then, bending forward and looking on the terrace where I was sitting with Doctor Nikitin and Yelpatievsky, he said: "What are you talking about?"

"Plehve."

"Plehve ... Plehve ...," he repeated musingly after a pause, as though he heard the name for the first time. Then he shook himself like a bird, and said, with a faint smile:

"To-day from early morning I have had a silly thing running in my head; someone once told me that he saw the following epitaph in a cemetery:

'Beneath this stone there rests Ivan Yegoriev;

A tanner by trade, he always wetted hides.

His work was honest, his heart good, but, behold,

He passed away, leaving his business to his wife.

He was not yet old and might still have done a lot of work.

But God took him away to the life of paradise on the night

Friday to Saturday in Passion week ...'

and something like that...." He was silent, and then, nodding his head and smiling faintly, added: "In human stupidity when it is not malicious, there is something very touching, even beautiful.... There always is."

They called us to come to dinner.

XXXVI

"I do not like people when they are drunk, but I know some who become interesting when they are tipsy, who acquire what is not natural to them in their sober state—wit, beauty of thought, alertness, and richness of language. In such cases I am ready to bless wine."

Suler tells how he was once walking with Leo Nicolayevitch in Tverskaya Street when Tolstoi noticed in the distance two soldiers of the Guards. The metal of their accoutrements shone in the sun; their spurs jingled; they kept step like one man; their faces, too, shone with the self-assurance of strength and youth.

Tolstoi began to grumble at them: "What pompous stupidity! Like animals trained by the whip...."

But when the guardsmen came abreast with him, he stopped, followed them caressingly with his eyes, and said enthusiastically: "How handsome! Old Romans, eh, Liovushka? Their strength and beauty! O Lord! How charming it is when man is handsome, how very charming!"

A LETTER

I have just posted a letter to you—telegrams have arrived telling of "Tolstoi's flight," and now once more one with you in thought I write again.

Probably all I want to say about the news will seem to you confused, perhaps even harsh and ill-tempered, but you will forgive me—I am feeling as though I had been gripped by the throat and was being strangled.

I had many long conversations with him; when he was living at Gaspra in the Crimea, I often went to him and he liked coming to me; I have studied his books lovingly; it seems to me that I have the right to say what I think of him, even if it be bold and differ widely from the general opinion. I know as well as others that no man is more worthy than he of the name of genius; more complicated, contradictory, and great in everything—yes, yes, in everything. Great—in some curious sense wide, indefinable by words—there is something in him which made me desire to cry aloud to everyone: "Look what a wonderful man is living on the earth." For he is, so to say, universally and above all a man, a man of mankind.

But what always repelled me in him was that stubborn despotic inclination to turn the life of Count Leo Nicolayevitch Tolstoi into "the saintly life of our blessed father, boyard Leo." As you know, he has for long intended to suffer; he expressed his regret to E. Soloviov, to Suler, that he had not succeeded, but he wanted to suffer simply, not out of a natural desire to test the resistance of his will, but with the obvious and, I repeat, the despotic intention of increasing the influence of his religious ideas, the weight of his teaching, in order to make his preaching irresistible, to make it holy in the eyes of man through his suffering, to force them to accept it; you understand, to force them. For he realizes that that preaching is not sufficiently convincing; in his diary you will, some day, read good instances of scepticism applied by him to his own preaching and personality. He knows that "martyrs and sufferers, with rare exceptions, are despots and tyrants"—he knows everything! And yet he says to himself, "Were I to suffer for my ideas they would have a greater influence." This in him always repelled me, for I cannot help feeling that it is an attempt to use violence to me—a desire to get hold of my conscience, to dazzle it with the glory of righteous blood, to put on my neck the yoke of a dogma.

He always greatly exalted immortality on the other side of life, but he preferred it on this side. A writer, national in the truest and most complete sense, he embodied in his great soul all the defects of his nation, all the mutilations caused us by the ordeals of our history; his misty preaching of "non-activity," of "non-resistance to evil"—the doctrine of passivism—this is all the unhealthy ferment of the old Russian blood, envenomed by Mongolian fatalism and almost chemically hostile to the West with its untiring creative labour, with its active and indomitable resistance to the evil of life. What is called Tolstoi's "anarchism," essentially and fundamentally, expresses our Slav anti-stateism, which, again, is really a national characteristic and desire, ingrained in our flesh from old times, to scatter nomadically. Up to now we have indulged that desire passionately, as you and everyone else know. We Russians know it, too, but we break away, always along the line of least resistance; we see that this is pernicious, but still we crawl further and further away from one another—and these mournful cockroach journeyings are called "the history of Russia," of a State which has been established almost incidentally, mechanically, to the surprise of the majority of its honest-minded citizens, by the forces of the Variags, Tartars, Baltic Germans, and petty constables. To their surprise, because all the time "scattering," and only when we reached places beyond which we could find nothing worse—for we could go no further—well, then we stopped and settled down. This is the lot, the destiny to which we are doomed—to settle in the snows and marshes by the side of the wild Erza, Tchood, Merey, Vess, and Muroma. Yet men arose who realized that light must come to us not from the East but from the West; and now he, the crown of our ancient history, wishes, consciously or unconsciously, to stretch himself like a vast mountain across our nation's path to Europe, to the active life which sternly demands of man the supreme effort of his spiritual forces. His attitude towards science is, too, certainly national: one sees magnificently reflected in him the old Russian village scepticism which comes from ignorance. Everything is national in him, and all his preaching is a reaction from the past, an atavism which we had already begun to shake off and overcome.

Think of his letter "The Intelligenzia, the State, the People," written in 1905—what a pernicious, malignant thing it is! You can hear in it the sectarian's "I told you so." At the time I wrote an answer to him, based on his own words to me that he had long since forfeited the right to speak of and on behalf of the Russian people, for I am a witness of his lack of desire to listen to and understand the people who came to talk to him soul to soul. My letter was bitter, and in the end I did not send it to him.

Well, now he is probably making his last assault in order to give to his ideas the highest possible significance. Like

Vassily Buslayev, he usually loved these assaults, but always so that he might assert his holiness and obtain a halo. That is dictatorial, although his teaching is justified by the ancient history of Russia and by his own sufferings of genius. Holiness is attained by flirting with sin, by subduing the will to live. People do desire to live, but he tries to persuade them: "That's all nonsense, our earthly life." It is very easy to persuade a Russian of this; he is a lazy creature who loves beyond anything else to find an excuse for his own inactivity. On the whole, of course, a Russian is not a Platon Karatayev, nor an Akim, nor a Bezonkhy, nor a Neklyudov; all these men were created by history and nature, not exactly on Tolstoi's pattern, he only improved on them in order more thoroughly to support his teaching. But, undeniably, Russia as a whole is—Tiulin above and Oblomov below. For the Tiulin above look at the year 1905, and for the Oblomov below look at Count A. N. Tolstoi, I. Bunin, look at everything round about you. Beasts and swindlers—we can leave them out of consideration, though our beast is exceedingly national—what a filthy coward he is for all his cruelty. Swindlers, of course, are international.

In Leo Nicolayevitch there is much which at times roused in me a feeling very like hatred, and this hatred fell upon my soul with crushing weight. His disproportionately overgrown individuality is a monstrous phenomenon, almost ugly, and there is in him something of Sviatogor, the bogatir, whom the earth can't hold. Yes, he is great. I am deeply convinced that, beyond all that he speaks of, there is much which he is silent about, even in his diary—he is silent, and, probably, will never tell it to anyone. That "something" only occasionally and in hints slipped through into his conversation, and hints of it are also to be found in the two note-books of his diary which he gave me and L. A. Sulerzhizky to read; it seems to me a kind of "negation of all affirmations," the deepest and most evil nihilism which has sprung from the soil of an infinite and unrelieved despair, from a loneliness which, probably, no one but he has experienced with such terrifying clearness. I often thought him to be a man who in the depths of his soul is stubbornly indifferent to people: he is so much above and beyond them that they seem to him like midges and their activities ridiculous and miserable. He has gone too far away from them into some desert, and there solitary, with the highest effort of all the force of his spirit, he closely examines into "the most essential," into death.

All his life he feared and hated death, all his life there throbbed in his soul the "Arsamaxian terror" —must he die? The whole world, all the earth looks toward him; from China, India, America, from everywhere living, throbbing threads stretch out to him; his soul is for all and for ever. Why should not Nature make an exception to her law, give to one man physical immortality—why not? He is certainly too rational and sensible to believe in miracles, but, on the other hand, he is a bogatir, an explorer, and, like a young recruit, wild and headstrong from fear and despair in face of the unknown barrack. I remember in Gaspra he read Leo Shestov's book Good and Evil in the Teaching of Nietzsche and Tolstoi, and, when Anton Tchekhov remarked that he did not like the book, Tolstoi said: "I thought it amusing. It's written swaggeringly, but it's all right and interesting. I'm sure I like cynics when they are sincere. Now he says: 'Truth is not wanted'; quite true, what should he want truth for? For he will die all the same."

And, evidently seeing that his words had not been understood, he added with a quick smile:—

"If a man has learned to think, no matter what he may think about;, he is always thinking of his own death. All philosophers were like that. And what truths can there be, if there is death?"

He went on to say that truth is the same for all —love of God; but on this subject he spoke coldly and wearily. After lunch on the terrace, he took up the book again, and, finding the passage, "Tolstoi, Dostoevsky, Nietzsche could not live without an answer to their questions, and for them any answer was better than none," he laughed and said:

"What a daring coiffeur; he says straight that I deceived myself, and that means that I deceived others too. That is the obvious conclusion...."

"Why coiffeur?" asked Suler.

"Well," he answered thoughtfully, "it just came into my mind—he is fashionable, chic, and I remembered the coiffeur from Moscow at a wedding of his peasant uncle in the village. He has the finest manners and he dances fashionably, and so he despises everyone."

I repeat this conversation, I think, almost literally; it is most memorable for me, and I even wrote it down, as I did many other things which struck me. Sulerzhizky and I wrote down many things which Tolstoi said, but Suler lost his notes when he came to me at Arsamas: he was habitually careless, and although he loved Leo Nicolayevitch like a woman, he behaved towards him rather strangely, almost like a superior. I have also mislaid my notes somewhere, and cannot find them; someone in Russia must have got them. I watched Tolstoi very attentively, because I was looking for—I am still looking for, and will until my death—a man with an active and a living faith. And also because once Anton Tchekhov, speaking of our lack of culture, complained:

"Goethe's words were all recorded, but Tolstoi's thoughts are being lost in the air. That, my dear fellow, is intolerably

Russian. After his death they will bestir themselves, will begin to write reminiscences, and will lie."

But to return to Shestov. "'It is impossible,' he says, 'to live looking at horrible ghosts,' but how does he know whether it's horrible or not? If he knew, if he saw ghosts, he would not write this nonsense, but would do something serious, what Buddha did all his life."

Someone remarked that Shestov was a Jew.

"Hardly," said Leo Nicolayevitch doubtfully.

"No, he is not like a Jew; there are no disbelieving Jews, you can't name one.... no."

It seemed sometimes as though this old sorcerer were playing with Death, coquetting with her, trying somehow to deceive her, saying: "I am not afraid of thee, I love thee, I long for thee."

And at the same time peering at Death with his keen little eyes: "What art thou like? What follows thee hereafter? Wilt thou destroy me altogether, or will something in me go on living?"

A strange impression used to be produced by his words: "I am happy, I am awfully happy, I am too happy." And then immediately afterwards: "To suffer." To suffer—that, too, was true in him; I don't doubt for a second that he, only half convalescent, would have been really glad to be put into prison, to be banished—in a word, to embrace a martyr's crown. Would not martyrdom probably in some measure justify death, make her more understandable, acceptable from the external, from the formal point of view? But he was never happy, never and nowhere; I am certain of that: neither "in the books of wisdom," nor "on the back of a horse," nor "in the arms of a woman" did he experience the full delights of "earthly paradise." He is too rational for that and knows life and people too well. Here are some more of his words:

"The Kaliph Abdurahman had during his life fourteen happy days, but I am sure I have not had so many. And this is because I have never lived—I cannot live—for myself, for my own self; I live for show, for people."

When we left, Anton Tchekhov said to me: "I don't believe that he was not happy." But I believe it. He was not. Though it is not true that he lived for show. Yes, what he himself did not need, he gave to people as though they were beggars; he liked to compel them, to compel them to read, walk, be vegetarians, love the peasants, and believe in the infallibility of the rational-religious reflections of Leo Tolstoi. People must be given something which will either satisfy or amuse them, and then let them be off. Let them leave a man in peace, to his habitual, tormenting, and sometimes cosy loneliness in face of the bottomless pit of the problem of "the essential."

All Russian preachers, with the exception of Avvakum and, perhaps, Tikhon Zadonsky, are cold men, for they did not possess an active and living faith. When I was writing Luka in The Lower Depths, I wanted to describe an old man like that: he is interested in "every solution," but not in people; coming inevitably in contact with them, he consoles them, but only in order that they may leave him in peace. And all the philosophy, all the preaching of such men, is alms bestowed by them with a veiled aversion, and there sounds behind their preaching words which are beggarly and melancholy: "Get out! Love God or your neighbour, but get out! Curse God, love the stranger, but leave me alone! Leave me alone, for I am a man and I am doomed to death."

Alas, so it is and so it will be. It could not and cannot be otherwise, for men have become worn out, exhausted, terribly separated, and they are all chained to a loneliness which dries up the soul. If Leo Nicolayevitch had had a reconciliation with the Church, it would not have at all surprised me. The thing would have had a logic of its own; all men are equally insignificant, even Archbishops. In fact, it would not have been a reconciliation, strictly speaking; for him personally the act would have been only logical: "I forgive those who hate me." It would have been a Christian act, and behind it there would have hidden a quick, ironical, little smile, which would be understood as the way in which a wise man retaliates on the fools.

What I write is not what I want to say; I cannot express it properly. There is a dog howling in my soul and I have a foreboding of some misfortune. Yes, newspapers have just arrived and it is already clear: you at home are beginning to "create a legend": idlers and good-for-nothings have gone on living and have now produced a saint. Only think how pernicious it is for the country just at this moment, when the heads of disillusioned men are bowed down, the souls of the majority empty, and the souls of the best full of sorrow. Lacerated and starving, they long for a legend. They long so much for alleviation of pain, for the soothing of torment. And they will create just what he desires, but what is not wanted—the life of a holy man and saint; but surely he is great and holy because he is a man, a madly and tormentingly beautiful man; a man of the whole of mankind. I am somehow contradicting myself in this, but it does not matter. He is a man seeking God, not for himself, but for men, so that God may leave him, the man, alone in the peace of the desert chosen by him. He gave us the Gospels in order that we might forget the contradictions in Christ; he simplified Christ's image, smoothing away the militant elements and bringing into the foreground the humble "will of Him that sent Him." No doubt Tolstoi's Gospel is the more easily accepted because it is "soothing to the malady" of the Russian people. He had to give them something, for they complain and trouble the earth with their groaning and distract him from "the essential." But War and Peace and all the other things of the same kind will not soothe the sorrow and despair of the grey Russian land. Of War and Peace he himself said: "Without false modesty, it is like the Iliad." M. Y. Tchaikovsky heard from his lips exactly the same appreciation of Childhood, Youth.

Journalists have just arrived from Naples; one even hurried from Rome. They ask me to say what I think of Tolstoi's "flight"—"flight" is the word they use. I would not talk to them. You, of course, understand that inwardly I am terribly disturbed; I do not want to see Tolstoi a saint; let him remain a sinner close to the heart of the all-sinful world, even close to the heart of each one of us. Poushkin and he—there is nothing more sublime or dearer to us.

Leo Tolstoi is dead.

A telegram came containing the commonest of words—is dead.

It struck me to the heart; I cried with pain and anger, and now, half crazy, I imagine him as I know and saw him—I am tormented by a desire to speak with him. I imagine him in his coffin—he lies like a smooth stone at the bottom of a stream, and in his grey beard, I am sure, is quietly hidden that aloof, mysterious, little smile. And at last his hands are folded peacefully—they have finished their hard task.

I remember his keen eyes—they saw everything through and through—and the movements of his fingers, as though they were perpetually modelling something out of the air, his talk, his jokes, his favourite peasant words, his elusive voice. And I see what a vast amount of life was embodied in the man, how inhumanly clever he was, how terrifying.

I once saw him as, perhaps, no one has ever seen him. I was walking over to him at Gaspra along the coast, and behind Yussupov's estate, on the shore among the stones I saw his smallish, angular figure in a grey, crumpled, ragged suit and crumpled hat. He was sitting with his head on his hands, the wind blowing the silvery hairs of his beard through his fingers: he was looking into the distance out to sea, and the little greenish waves rolled up obediently to his feet and fondled them as though they were telling something about themselves to the old magician. It was a day of sun and cloud, and the shadows of the clouds glided over the stones, and with the stones the old man grew now bright and now dark. The boulders were large, riven by cracks, and covered with smelling sea-weed: there had been a high tide. He, too, seemed to me like an old stone come to life, who knows all the beginnings and the ends of things, who considers when and what will be the end of the stones, the grasses of the earth, of the waters of the sea, and of the whole universe from the pebble to the sun. And the sea is part of his soul, and everything around him comes from him, out of him. In the musing motionlessness of the old man I felt something fateful, magical, something which went down into the darkness beneath him and stretched up, like a searchlight, into the blue emptiness above the earth -as though it were he, his concentrated will, which was drawing the waves to him and repelling them, which was ruling the movements of cloud and shadow, which was stirring the stones to life. Suddenly, in a moment of madness, I felt it is possible, he will get up, wave his hand, and the sea will become solid and glassy, the stones will begin to move and cry out, everything around him will come to life, acquire a voice, and speak in their different voices of themselves, of him, against him. I cannot express in words what I felt rather than thought at that moment; in my soul there was joy and fear, and then everything blended in one happy thought: "I am not an orphan on the earth so long as this man lives on it."

Then I walked on tip-toe away in order that the pebbles might not scrunch under my feet, not wishing to distract his thoughts. And now I feel I am an orphan, I cry as I write—never before have I cried so unconsolably and in such bitter despair. I do not know whether I loved him; but does it matter, love of him or hatred? He always roused in me sensations and agitations which were enormous, fantastic; even the unpleasant and hostile feelings which he aroused were of a kind not to oppress, but rather to explode the soul: they made it more sensitive and capacious. He was grand when, with his boots scraping over the ground, as though he were imperiously smoothing its unevenness, he suddenly appeared from somewhere, from behind a door or out of some corner, and came towards you with the short, light, quick step of a man accustomed to walk a great deal on the earth. With his thumbs in his belt he would stop for a second, looking round quickly with a comprehensive glance, a glance which at once took in anything new and instantly absorbed the meaning of everything.

"How do you do?"

I always translated these words into: "How do you do? There's pleasure for me, and for you there's not much sense in it—but still, how do you do?"

He would come out looking rather small, and immediately everyone round him would become smaller than he. A peasant's beard, rough but extraordinary hands, simple clothes, all this external, comfortable democratism deceived many people, and I often saw how Russians who judge people by their clothes—an old slavish habit—began to pour out a stream of their odious "frankness," which is more properly called "the familiarity of the pig-sty."

"Ah, you are one of us! That's what you are. At last, by God's grace, I am face to face with the greatest son of our native land. Hail for ever. I bow low to you."

That is a sample of Muscovite Russian, simple and hearty, and here is another, but "free-thinkerish":

"Leo Nicolayevitch, though I disagree with your religious-philosophical views, I deeply respect in your person the greatest of artists."

And suddenly, under his peasant's beard, under his democratic crumpled blouse, there would rise the old Russian *bariny* the grand aristocrat: then the noses of the simple-hearted visitor, educated and all the rest, instantly became blue with intolerable cold. It was pleasant to see this creature of the purest blood, to watch the noble grace of his gestures, the proud reserve of his speech, to hear the exquisite pointedness of his murderous words. He showed just as much of the *barin* as was needed for these serfs, and when they called out the *barin* in Tolstoi it appeared naturally and easily and crushed them so that they shrivelled up and whined.

One day I was returning from Yasnaya Polyana to Moscow with one of these "simple-hearted" Russians, a Moscow man, and for a long time he could not recover his breath, but kept on smiling woefully and repeating in astonishment: "Well, well, that was a cold bath. He's severe ... pooh!"

And in the middle of it all he exclaimed, apparently with regret: "And I thought he was really an anarchist. Everyone keeps on saying: Anarchist, anarchist,' and I believe it...."

The man was a large, rich manufacturer, with a great belly, and a face the colour of raw meat—why did he want Tolstoi to be an anarchist? One of the "profound mysteries" of the Russian soul!

When Leo Nicolayevitch wished to please, he could do so more easily than a clever and beautiful woman. Imagine a company of people of all kinds sitting in his room: the Grand Duke Nicolay Mikhailovitch, the house-painter Ilya, a social-democrat from Yalta, the stundist Patzuk, a musician, a German, the manager of the estates of Countess Kleinmichel, the poet Bulgakov, and all look at him with the same enamoured eyes. He explains to them the teaching of Lao-Tse, and he seems to me an extraordinary man-orchestra, possessing the faculty of playing several instruments at the same time, a brass trumpet, a drum, harmonium, and flute. I used to look at him just as the others did. And now I long to see him once more—and I shall never see him again.

Journalists have come asserting that a telegram has been received in Rome "denying the rumour of Tolstoi's death." They bustled and chattered, redundantly expressing their sympathy with Russia. The Russian newspapers leave no room for doubt.

To lie to him, even out of pity, was impossible; even when he was seriously ill, one could not pity him. It would be banal to pity a man like him. They ought to be taken care of, cherished, not loaded with the wordy dust of worn-out, soulless words.

He used to ask: "You don't like me?" and one had to answer: "No, I don't."

"You don't love me?"—"No, to-day I don't love you."

In his questions he was merciless, in his answers reserved, as becomes a wise man.

He used to speak with amazing beauty of the past, and particularly of Turgeniev; of Fet always with a good-natured smile and always something amusing, of Nekrassov coldly and sceptically; but of all writers exactly as if they were his children and he, the father, knew all their faults, and—there you are!

He would point out their faults before their merits, and every time he blamed someone it seemed to me that he was giving alms to his listeners because of their poverty; to listen to him then made one feel awkward, one's eyes fell before his sharp little smile and—nothing remained in one's memory.

Once he argued fiercely that G. Y. Uspensky wrote in the Tula language, and had no talent at all. And later I heard him say to Anton Pavlovitch Tchekhov: "He (Uspensky) is a writer! In the power of his sincerity he recalls Dostoevsky, only Dostoevsky went in for politics and coquetted, while Uspensky is more simple and sincere. If he had believed in God, he would have been a sectarian."

"But you said he was a Tula writer and had no talent."

He drew his shaggy brows down over his eyes and said: "He wrote badly. What kind of language does he use? There are more punctuation marks than words. Talent is love. One who loves is talented. Look at lovers, they are all talented."

Of Dostoevsky he spoke reluctantly, constrainedly, evading or repressing something: "He ought to have made himself acquainted with the teaching of Confucius or the Buddhists; that would have calmed him down. That is the chief thing which everyone should know. He was a man of rebellious flesh; when angry, bumps would suddenly rise on his bald head; and his ears would move. He felt a great deal, but he thought poorly; it is from the Fourierists, from Butashevitch and the others, that he learnt to think. And afterwards all his life long he hated them. There was something Jewish in his blood. He was suspicious without reason, ambitious, heavy and unfortunate. It is curious that he is so much read. I can't understand why. It is all painful and useless, because all those Idiots, Adolescents, Raskolnikovs, and the rest of them, they are not real; it is all much simpler, more understandable. It's a pity people don't read Lieskov, he's a real writer—have you read him?"

"Yes, I like him very much, especially his language."

"He knew the language marvellously, even the tricks. Strange that you should like him; somehow you are not Russian, your thoughts are not Russian -is it all right, you're not hurt at my saying that r I am an old man, and, perhaps, I can no longer understand modern literature, but it seems to me that it is all not Russian. They begin to write a curious kind of verse; I don't know what these poems are or what they mean. One has to learn to write poetry from Poushkin, Tiutchev, Fet. Now you"—he turned to Tchekhov—"you are Russian. Yes, very, very Russian."

And smiling affectionately, he put his hand on Tchekhov's shoulder; and the latter became uncomfortable and began in a low voice to mutter something about his bungalow and the Tartars.

He loved Tchekhov, and, when he looked at him, his eyes were tender and seemed almost to stroke Anton Pavlovitch's face. Once, when Anton Pavlovitch was walking on the lawn with Alexandra Lvovna, Tolstoi, who at the time was still ill and was sitting in a chair on the terrace, seemed to stretch towards them, saying in a whisper: "Ah, what a beautiful, magnificent man: modest and quiet like a girl! And he walks like a girl. He's simply wonderful."

One evening, in the twilight, half closing his eyes and moving his brows, he read a variant of the scene in Father Sergius, where the woman goes to seduce the hermit: he read it through to the end, and then, raising his head and shutting his eyes, he said distinctly: "The old man wrote it well, well."

It came out with such amazing simplicity, his pleasure in its beauty was so sincere, that I shall never forget the delight which it gave me at the time, a delight which I could not—did not know how to express, but which I could only suppress by a tremendous effort. My heart stopped beating for a moment, and then everything around me seemed to become fresh and revivified.

One must have heard him speak in order to understand the extraordinary, indefinable beauty of his speech; it was, in a sense, incorrect, abounding in repetitions of the same word, saturated with village simplicity. The effect of his words did not come only from the intonation and the expression of his face, but from the play and light in his eyes, the most eloquent eyes I have ever seen. In his two eyes Leo Nicolayevitch possessed a thousand eyes.

Once Suler, Sergey Lvovitch, Tchekhov, and someone else, were sitting in the park and talking about women; he listened in silence for a long time, and then suddenly said:

"And I will tell the truth about women, when I have one foot in the grave—I shall tell it, jump into my coffin, pull the lid over me, and say, 'Do what you like now.'" The look he gave us was so wild, so terrifying that we all fell silent for a while.

He had in him, I think, the inquisitive, mischievous wildness of a Vaska Buslayev, and also something of the stubbornness of soul of the Protopop Avvakum, while above or at his side lay hidden the scepticism of a Tchaadayev. The Avvakumian element harried and tormented with its preachings the artist in him; the Novgorod wildness upset Shakespeare and Dante, while the Tchaadayevian element scoffed at his soul's amusements and, by the way, at its agonies. And the old Russian man in him dealt a blow at science and the State, the Russian driven to the passivity of anarchism by the barrenness of all his efforts to build up a more human life.

Strange! This Buslayev characteristic in Tolstoi was perceived through some mysterious intuition by Olaf Gulbranson, the caricaturist of Simplicissimus: look closely at his drawing and you will see how startlingly he has got the likeness of the real Tolstoi, what intellectual daring there is in that face with its veiled and hidden eyes, for which nothing is sacred and which believe "neither in a sneeze, nor a dream, nor the cawing of a bird."

The old magician stands before me, alien to all, a solitary traveller through all the deserts of thought in search of an all-embracing truth which he has not found—I look at him and, although I feel sorrow for the loss, I feel pride at having seen the man, and that pride alleviates my pain and grief.

It was curious to see Leo Nicolayevitch among "Tolstoyans"; there stands a noble belfry and its bell sounds untiringly over the whole world, while round about run tiny, timorous dogs whining at the bell and distrustfully looking askance at one another as though to say, "Who howled best?" I always thought that these people infected the Yassnaya Polyana house, as well as the great house of Countess Panin, with a spirit of hypocrisy, cowardice, mercenary and self-seeking pettiness and legacy-hunting. The "Tolstoyans" have something in common with those friars who wander in all the dark corners of Russia, carrying with them dogs' bones and passing them off as relics, selling "Egyptian darkness" and the "little tears of Our Lady." One of these apostles, I remember, at Yassnaya Polyana refused to eat eggs so as not to wrong the hens, but at Tula railway-station he greedily devoured meat, saying: "The old fellow does exaggerate."

Nearly all of them like to moan and kiss one another; they all have boneless perspiring hands and lying eyes. At the same time they are practical fellows and manage their earthly affairs cleverly.

Leo Nicolayevitch, of course, well understood the value of the "Tolstoyans," and so did Sulerzhizky, whom Tolstoi loved tenderly and whom he always spoke of with a kind of youthful ardour and fervour. Once one of those "Tolstoyans" at Yassnaya Polyana explained eloquently how happy his life had become and how pure his soul after he accepted Tolstoy's teaching. Leo Nicolayevitch leant over and said to me in a low voice: "He's lying all the time, the rogue, but he does it to please me...."

Many tried to please him, but I did not observe that they did it well or with any skill. He rarely spoke to me on his usual subjects of universal forgiveness, loving one's neighbour, the Gospels, and Buddhism, evidently because he realized at once that all that would not "go down" with me. I greatly appreciated this.

When he liked he could be extraordinarily charming, sensitive, and tactful; his talk was fascinatingly simple and elegant, but sometimes it was painfully unpleasant to listen to him. I always disliked what he said about women—it was unspeakably "vulgar," and there was in his words something artificial, insincere, and at the same time very personal. It seemed as if he had once been hurt, and could neither forget nor forgive. The evening when I first got to know him, he took me into his study—it was at Khamovniki in Moscow—and, making me sit opposite to him, began to talk about Varienka Oliessova and of Twenty-Six and One. I was overwhelmed by his tone and lost my head, he spoke so plainly and brutally, arguing that in a healthy girl chastity is not natural. "If a girl who has turned fifteen is healthy, she desires to be touched and embraced. Her mind is still afraid of the unknown and of what she does not understand -that is what they call chastity and purity. But her flesh is already aware that the incomprehensible is right, lawful, and, in spite of the mind, it demands fulfilment of the law. Now you describe Varienka Oliessova as healthy, but her feelings are anaemic—that is not true to life."

Then he began to speak about the girl in Twenty-six and One, using a stream of indecent words with a simplicity which seemed to me cynical and even offended me. Later I came to see that he used unmentionable words only because he found them more precise and pointed, but at the time it was unpleasant to me to listen to him. I made no reply, and suddenly he became attentive and kindly and began asking me about my life, what I was studying, and what I read.

"I am told that you are very well read; is that true? Is Korolenko a musician?"

"I believe not; but I'm not sure."

"You don't know? Do you like his stories?"

"I do very much."

"It is the contrast. He is lyrical and you haven't got that. Have you read Weltmann?"

"Yes."

"Isn't he a good writer, clever, exact, and with no exaggeration? He is sometimes better than Gogol. He knew Balzac. And Gogol imitated Marlinsky."

When I said that Gogol was probably influenced by Hoffmann, Stern, and perhaps Dickens, he glanced at me and asked: "Have you read that somewhere? No? It isn't true. Gogol hardly knew Dickens. But you must clearly have read a great deal: now look here, it's dangerous. Kolzov ruined himself by it."

When he accompanied me to the door, he embraced and kissed me and said: "You are a real mouzhik. You will find it difficult to live among writers, but never mind, don't be afraid, always say what you feel even if it be rude—it doesn't matter. Sensible people will understand."

I had two impressions from this first meeting: I was glad and proud to have seen Tolstoi, but his conversation reminded me a little of an examination, and in a sense I did not see in him the author of Cossacks, Kholstomier, War and Peace, but a barin who, making allowances for me, considered it necessary to speak to me in the common language, the language of the street and market-place. That upset my idea of him, an idea which was deeply rooted and had become dear to me.

It was at Yassnaya Polyana that I saw him again. It was an overcast, autumn day with a drizzle of rain, and he put on a heavy overcoat and high leather boots and took me for a walk in the birch wood. He jumped the ditches and pools like a boy, shook the rain-drops off the branches, and gave me a superb account of how Fet had explained Schopenhauer to him in this wood. He stroked the damp, satin trunks of the birches lovingly with his hand and said: "Lately I read a poem—

The mushrooms are gone, but in the hollows
Is the heavy smell of mushroom dampness....
Very good, very true."

Suddenly a hare got up under our feet. Leo Nicolayevitch started up excited, his face lit up, and he whooped like a real old sportsman. Then, looking at me with a curious little smile, he broke into a sensible, human laugh. He was wonderfully charming at that moment.

Another time he was looking at a hawk in the park: it was hovering over the cattle-shed, making wide circles suspended in the air, moving its wings very slightly as if undecided whether or not the moment to strike had come. Leo Nicolayevitch stood up shading his eyes with his hand and murmured with excitement: "The rogue is going for our chickens. Now, now ... it's coming ... O, he's afraid. The groom is there, isn't he? I'll call the groom...."

And he shouted to the groom. When he shouted, the hawk was scared, swept upwards, swung away, and disappeared. Leo Nicolayevitch sighed, apparently reproaching himself, and said: "I should not have shouted; he would have struck all the same...."

Once in telling him about Tiflis, I mentioned the name of V. V. Flerovsky-Bervi. "Did you know him?" Leo Nicolayevitch asked with interest: "Tell me, what is he like?"

I told him about Flerovsky: tall, long-bearded, thin, with very large eyes; how he used to wear a long, sail-cloth blouse, and how, armed with a bundle of rice, cooked in red wine, tied in his belt, and an enormous linen umbrella, he wandered with me on the mountain paths of Trans-Caucasia; how once on a narrow path we met a buffalo and prudently retreated, threatening the brute with the open umbrella, and, every time we stepped back, in danger of falling over the precipice. Suddenly I noticed that there were tears in Tolstoi's eyes, and this confused me and I stopped.

"Never mind," he said, "go on, go on. It's pleasure at hearing about a good man. I imagined him just like that, unique. Of all the radicals he is the most mature and clever; in his Alphabet he proves conclusively that all our civilization is barbarian, that culture is the work of the peaceful and weak, not the strong, nations, and that the struggle for existence is a lying invention by which it is sought to justify evil. You, of course, don't agree with this? But Daudet agrees, you know, you remember his Paul Astier?"

"But how would you reconcile Flerovsky's theory, say, with the part played by the Normans in the history of Europe?"

"The Normans? That's another thing."

If he did not want to answer, he would always say "That's another thing."

It always seemed to me—and I do not think I was mistaken—that Leo Nicolayevitch was not very fond of talking about literature, but was vitally interested in the personality of an author. The questions: "Do you know him? What is he like? Where was he born?" I often heard in his mouth. And nearly all his opinions would throw some curious light upon a man.

Of V.K. he said thoughtfully: "He is not a Great Russian, and so he must see our life better and more truly than we do." Of Anton Tchekhov, whom he loved dearly: "His medicine gets in his way; if he were not a doctor, he would be a still better writer." Of one of the younger writers: "He pretends to be an Englishman, and in that character a Moscow man has the least success." To me he once said: "You are an inventor: all these Kuvaldas of yours are inventions." When I answered that Kuvalda had been drawn from life, he said: "Tell me, where did you see him?"

He laughed heartily at the scene in the court of the Kazan magistrate, Konovalov, where I had first seen the man whom I described under the name of Kuvalda. "Blue blood," he said, wiping the tears from his eyes, "that's it—blue blood. But how splendid, how amusing. You tell it better than you write it. Yes, you are an inventor, a romantic, you must confess."

I said that probably all writers are to some extent inventors, describing people as they would like to see them in life; I also said that I liked active people who desire to resist the evil of life by every means, even violence.

"And violence is the chief evil," he exclaimed, taking me by the arm. "How will you get out of that contradiction, inventor? Now your My Travelling Companion isn't invented—it's good just because it isn't invented. But when you think, you beget knights, all Amadises and Siegfrieds."

I remarked that as long as we live in the narrow sphere of our anthropomorphous and unavoidable "travelling companions," we build everything on quicksands and in a hostile medium.

He smiled and nudged me slightly with his elbow: "From that very, very dangerous conclusions can be drawn. You are a questionable Socialist. You are a romantic, and romantics must be monarchists—they always have been."

"And Hugo?"

"Hugo? That's another thing. I don't like him, a noisy man."

He often asked me what I was reading, and always reproached me if I had chosen, in his opinion, a bad book.

"Gibbon is worse than Kostomarov; one ought to read Mommsen, he's very tedious, but it's all so solid."

When he heard that the first book I ever read was The Brothers Semganno, he even got angry:

"Now, you see—a stupid novel. That's what has spoilt you. The French have three writers, Stendhal, Balzac, Flaubert; and, well, perhaps Maupassant, though Tchekhov is better than he. The Goncourts are mere clowns, they only pretended to be serious. They had studied life from books written by inventors like themselves, and they thought it a serious business; but it was of no use to a soul."

I disagreed with this opinion, and it irritated Leo Nicolayevitch a little; he could barely stand contradiction, and sometimes his opinions were strange and capricious.

"There is no such thing as degeneration," he said once. "The Italian Lombroso invented it, and after him comes the Jew Nordau, screaming like a parrot. Italy is the land of charlatans and adventurers: only Arentinos, Casanovas, Cagliostros, and the like are born there."

"And Garibaldi?"

"That's politics; that's another thing."

To a whole series of facts, taken from the life of the merchant-class families in Russia, he answered: "But it's untrue; it's only written in clever books."

I told him the actual history of three generations of a merchant family which I had known, a history in which the law of degeneration had acted with particular mercilessness. Then he began excitedly tugging at my arm and encouraging me to write about it: "Now that's true. I know it; there are two families like that in Tula. It ought to be written. A long novel, written concisely, do you see? You must do it." His eyes flashed.

"But then there will be knights, Leo Nicolayevitch."

"Don't. This is really serious. The one who is going to be a monk and pray for the whole family —it's wonderful. That's real: you sin and I will go and expiate your sin by prayer. And the other, the weary one, the money-loving founder of the family—that's true too. And he's a drunken, profligate beast, and loves everyone, and suddenly commits murder—ah, it's good. It should be written, among thieves and beggars you must not look for heroes, you really mustn't. Heroes—that's a lie and invention; there are simply people, people, and nothing else."

He often pointed out exaggerations in my stories, but once, speaking of Dead Souls, he said, smiling good-naturedly:

"We are all of us terrible inventors. I myself, when I write, suddenly feel pity for some character, and then I give him some good quality or take a good quality away from someone else, so that in comparison with the others he may not appear too black." And then in the stern tones of an inexorable judge: "That's why I say that art is a lie, an arbitrary sham, harmful for people. One writes not what real life is, but simply what one thinks of life oneself. What good is that to anyone, how I see that tower or sea or Tartar—what interest or use is there in it?"

[At times his thoughts and feelings seemed to me capriciously, even deliberately, perverse, but what particularly struck and upset men was just the stern directness of his thought, like Job, the fearless questioner of the cruel God. He said:

"I was walking one day on the road to Kiev, about the end of May; the earth was a paradise; everything rejoiced; the birds sang; the bees hummed; the sunshine and everything seemed so happy, humane, splendid. I was moved to tears; I felt myself a bee to whom are given the best flowers, and I felt God close to my soul. And suddenly I saw by the roadside a man and woman, pilgrims; they were lying together, both grey, dirty, and old —they writhed like worms, made noises, murmured, and the sun pitilessly lighted up their naked blue legs and wizened bodies. It struck such a blow to my soul. Lord, thou creator of beauty, how art thou not ashamed? I felt utterly wretched——

"Yes, you see what things happen. Nature—the devout considered her the work of the devil—cruelly and mockingly torments man; she takes away the power and leaves the desire. All men with a living soul experience that. Only man is made to experience the whole shame and horror of that torment, given to him in his flesh. We carry it in ourselves as an inevitable punishment—a punishment for what sin?"

While he said this the look in his eyes changed strangely, now childishly plaintive, now hard and stern and bright. His lips trembled, his moustache bristled. When he had finished, he took a handkerchief from the pocket of his blouse and wiped his face hard, though it was dry. Then he smoothed his beard with the knotted fingers of his strong peasant's hand, and repeated gently: "Yes, for what sin?"]

Once I was walking with him on the lower road from Dyulbev to Ai-Todor On; he was walking with the light step of a young man, when he said to me more nervously than was usual with him: "The flesh should be the obedient dog of the spirit, running to do its bidding; but we—how do we live? The flesh rages and riots, and the spirit follows it helpless and miserable."

He rubbed his chest hard over the heart, raised his eyebrows, and then, remembering something, went on: "One autumn in Moscow in an alley near the Sukhariov Gate I once saw a drunken woman lying in the gutter. A stream of filthy water flowed from the yard of a house right under her neck and back. She lay in that cold liquid, muttering, shivering, wriggling her body in the wet, but she could not get up."

He shuddered, half closed his eyes, shook his head, and went on gently: "Let's sit down here.... It's the most horrible and disgusting thing, a drunken woman. I wanted to help her get up, but I couldn't; I felt such a loathing; she was so slippery and slimy—I felt that if I'd touched her, I could not have washed my hand clean for a month —horrible. And on the curb sat a bright, grey-eyed boy, the tears running down his cheeks: he was sobbing and repeating wearily and helplessly: 'Mu-um ... mu-um-my ... do get up.' She would move her arms, grunt, lift her head, and again—bang went her neck into the filth."

He was silent, and then looking round, he repeated almost in a whisper: "Yes, yes, horrible. You've seen many drunken women? Many—my God! You, you must not write about that, you mustn't."

"Why?"

He looked straight into my eyes and smiling repeated: "Why?" Then thoughtfully and slowly he said: "I don't know. It just slipped out ... it's a shame to write about filth. But yet why not write about it? Yes, it's necessary to write all about everything, everything."

Tears came into his eyes. He wiped them away, and, smiling, he looked at his handkerchief, while the tears again ran down his wrinkles. "I am crying," he said. "I am an old man. It cuts me to the heart when I remember something horrible."

And very gently touching me with his elbow, he said: "You, too—you will have lived your life, and everything will remain exactly as it was, and then you, too, will cry worse than I, more streamingly,' as the peasant women say. And everything must be written about, everything; otherwise that bright little boy might be hurt, he might reproach us—'it's untrue, it's not the whole truth,' he will say. He's strict for the truth."

Suddenly he gave himself a shake and said in a kind voice: "Now, tell me a story; you tell them well. Something about a child, about your childhood. It's not easy to believe that you were once a child. You are a strange creature, exactly as if you were born grown-up. In your ideas there is a good deal of the child-like and the immature, but you know more than enough of life—and one cannot ask for more. Well, tell me a story....'

He lay down comfortably upon the bare roots of a pine tree and watched the ants moving busily among the grey spines.

In the South, which, with its self-asserting luxuriance and flaunting, unbridled vegetation, seems so strangely incongruous to a man from the North, he, Leo Tolstoi—even his name speaks of his inner power—seemed a small man, but knitted and knotted out of very strong roots deep in the earth —in the flaunting scenery of the Crimea, I say, he was at once both out of place and in his place. He seemed a very ancient man, master of all his surroundings—a master-builder who, after centuries of absence, has arrived in the mansion built by him. He has forgotten a great deal which it contains; much is new to him; everything is as it should be, and yet not entirely so, and he has at once to find out what is amiss and why it is amiss.

He walked the roads and paths with a businesslike, quick step of the skilled explorer of the earth, and with sharp eyes, from which neither a single pebble nor a single thought could hide itself, he looked, measured, tested, compared. And he scattered about him the living seeds of indomitable thoughts. He said to Suler once: "You, Liovushka, read nothing which is not good out of self-conceit, while Gorky reads a lot which is not good, because he distrusts himself. I write much which is not good, because of an old man's ambition, a desire that all should think as I do. Of course, I think it is good, and Gorky thinks it is not good, and you think nothing at all; you simply blink and watch what you may clutch. One day you will clutch something which does not belong to you—it has happened to you before. You will put your claws into it, hold on for a bit, and when it begins to get loose, you won't try to stop it. Tchekhov has a superb story, The Darling—you are rather like her."

"In what?" asked Suler, laughing.

"You can love well, but to choose—no, you can't, and you will waste yourself on trifles."

"Is everyone like that?"

"Everyone?" Leo Nicolayevitch repeated.

"No, not everyone."

And suddenly he asked me, exactly as if he were dealing me a blow: "Why don't you believe in God?"

"I have no faith, Leo Nicolayevitch."

"It is not true. By nature you are a believer, and you cannot get on without God. You will realize it one day. Your disbelief comes from obstinacy, because you have been hurt: the world is not what you would like it to be. There are also some people who do not believe out of shyness; it happens with young people; they adore some woman, but don't want to show it from fear that she won't understand, and also from lack of courage. Faith, like love, requires courage and daring. One has to say to oneself 'I believe,' and everything will come right, everything will appear as you want it, it will explain itself to you and attract you. Now, you love much, and faith is only a greater love: you must love still more, and then your love will turn to faith. When one loves a woman, she is, unfailingly, the best woman on earth, and each loves the best woman, and that is faith. A nonbeliever cannot love: to-day he falls in love with one woman, and next year with another. The souls of such men are tramps living barren lives—that is not good. But you were born a believer, and it is no use thwarting yourself. Well, you may say beauty? And what is beauty? The highest and most perfect is God."

He hardly ever spoke to me on this subject, and its seriousness and the suddenness of it rather overwhelmed me. I was silent.

He was sitting on the couch with his legs drawn up under him, and breaking into a triumphant little smile and shaking his finger at me, he said: "You won't get out of this by silence, no."

And I, who do not believe in God, looked at him for some reason very cautiously and a little timidly, I looked and thought: "The man is godlike."